TV CAPTURES TERRORISM ON
SEPTEMBER 11

An Augmented Reading Experience

by Emma Carlson Berne

Content Adviser: Alan Schroeder, Professor,
School of Journalism, Northeastern University

COMPASS POINT BOOKS
a capstone imprint

Compass Point Books are published by Capstone Press,
1710 Roe Crest Drive, North Mankato, Minnesota 56003
www.mycapstone.com

Editorial Credits
Michelle Bisson, editor; Tracy McCabe, designer; Svetlana Zhurkin, media researcher; Kathy
McColley, production specialist; Kathleen Baxter, library consultant

Photo Credits
AP Photo: APTN, 25, Gulnara Samoilova, 37; FEMA News Photo: Andrea Booher, 46, 57 (top
right); Getty Images: AFP/David Maxwell, 42, FBI, 23, Gamma-Rapho/Michel Setboun, 13,
Mario Tama, 9, 40, 48, Photo courtesy of the Sherburne County Sheriffs Office, 21, Roll Call/
Mark F. Sypher, 51; Newscom: Abaca/Balkis Press, 17, 19, Levine Roberts Photography/Frances
M. Roberts, 20, Reuters/Hyungwon Kang, 12, Reuters/Jeff Christensen, 30, 31, Reuters/Larry
Downing, 44, 57 (top left), Reuters/Shannon Stapleton, 7, 11, 54, Reuters/Win McNamee, 15,
Zuma Press/Uppa, 33; Reuters: Sara K. Schwittek, cover, 28; Shutterstock: Anthony Correia, 35,
45, Eo naya, 52, 57 (bottom), Ken Tannenbaum, 5, 55 (top); U.S. Navy: Photographer's Mate
3rd Class Carol Warden, 49, Photographer's Mate Master Chief Terry Cosgrove, 56; Wikipedia: U.S.
Air Force/Tech. Sgt. Cedric H. Rudisill, 39, 55 (bottom)

Content Adviser: Alan Schroeder, Professor, Northeastern School of Journalism

Acknowledgements: In the writing of this book, I drew many times on the excellent 9/11
Television News Archive, created and maintained by the Internet Archive digital library, as well
as the collection *Covering Catastrophe: Broadcast Journalists Report September 11*, by Allison
Gilbert, Phil Hirschkorn, Melinda Murphy, Robyn Walensky, and Mitchell Stephens (Chicago:
Bonus Books, 2002.) I am grateful to these resources and their authors and editors.

Library of Congress Cataloging-in-Publication Data
Cataloging-in-publication information is on file with the Library of Congress.
ISBN 978-0-7565-5824-6 (library binding)
ISBN 978-0-7565-5828-4 (paperback)
ISBN 978-0-7565-5832-1 (ebook pdf)

Download the Capstone 4D app!

- Ask an adult to download the Capstone 4D app.

- Scan the cover and stars inside the book for additional content.

When you scan a spread, you'll find fun extra stuff
to go with this book! You can also find these things
on the web at www.capstone4D.com using the
password: twintowers.58338

Printed and bound in the USA.
PA017

TABLEOFCONTENTS

ChapterOne
UNEXPECTED ON A CLEAR BLUE DAY

Tracy Ullman is on NBC's *Today* show at 8:00 a.m. The British comedian laughs as she greets fans outside NBC's New York studio. At 8:40 a.m. *Today* show host Katie Couric interviews singer Harry Belafonte. They discuss a new project of Belafonte's while seated in a comfortable, book-lined studio. At 8:49 a.m. co-host Matt Lauer talks about a new biography of Howard Hughes with the book's author, Richard Hack.

The morning is going as planned. And then it isn't.

There is a breaking news story, Lauer announces. They don't have details yet. A plane has crashed into the World Trade Center, Couric reports. The camera shows the North Tower with smoke billowing from a hole near the top. It stands out alone against the skyline, outlined in the cloudless, blue sky. The smoke pouring from the hole in the building is rich, black, pillowy, and foamy. The anchors are concerned. They—along with everyone else—think it's an accident. For 9 minutes, NBC shows live footage of the North Tower standing, smoking. The anchors interview people on the street who call in, and who describe to them in detail what they are seeing. It could be a terrorist act, the anchors speculate.

At 9:02 a.m., on live TV, a silvery object appears at the corner of the camera. The home viewer can

When a plane crashed into the World Trade Center, everyone was caught by surprise.

see the object before the TV anchors can. The object is an airplane—a jetliner. Silently, like a silver arrow, it flies straight and low and disappears behind the North Tower. The anchors are still talking about the first hit. Then the reporter yells. There has been another hit.

Orange and black fire is seen at the corner of the screen. Quickly, the camera switches angles. Flames are shrouding the side of the South Tower, as is black smoke. The audience can hear the crew in the newsroom gasp.

The news anchors, off-camera, are calm. They show the image of a jet flying into the South Tower and a fireball exploding again and again. Could it be terrorism? Could there be air-traffic control problems? No one knows. The cameras show only the smoking, burning towers of the World Trade Center. They never cut away. There are no commercials. Another reporter is on the line. It is 9:40 a.m. A blast of some kind has hit the Pentagon in Washington, D.C.

9:59 a.m. The anchors are recounting to the audience that New York City has been immobilized. Then, as the camera keeps its steady gaze trained on the smoking towers, something new happens. The top of the South Tower seems to disintegrate in front of the viewers' eyes. While the anchors talk, the audience watches as the tower, with a sort of smooth grace, silently collapses, seeming to move downward with swift precision. Dust and smoke foam up around it as silvery ribbons of dust and smoke arch up from the explosion and fall to earth until all that is left is hidden by mountainous gray clouds. A chunk of the building has fallen away, the anchors say. They are wrong. It is the entire South Tower. It has not fallen

A chunk of the building has fallen away, the anchors say. They are wrong. It is the entire South Tower.

Smoke and debris filled the air after the South Tower collapsed.

away. It has collapsed. "We can only hope the area has been evacuated," Couric says. But it hasn't. All told, 624 people will die in the South Tower.

By 10:03 a.m. the anchors are using the word *terrorism*. Half an hour earlier, at 9:30 a.m., President George W. Bush appears on television from Sarasota, Florida, and refers to the attacks as an "apparent terrorist attack." There is no question now that this is no accident. The planes have been hijacked.

The anchors' voices are sober and controlled. Wider camera shots taken from the water show Lower Manhattan enveloped in dense clouds of ground level smoke. The anchors tell the audience that the State Department in Washington has been evacuated. The camera shifts to the Pentagon, where fire hoses spray long jets onto the charred remains of the outer wall. The anchors talk about traffic, about bridge closures. Then at 10:28 a.m. the camera shifts again. The eerily calm voices of the anchors tell the audience that the North Tower of the World Trade Center has collapsed. They show the footage. The tower, with its gaping black wound at the top, falls in on itself, sending forth billows of black smoke, and odd, glittering shards all around—office paper, blown from all the offices. The sight is stunning, unbelievable. It takes place in the eerie calm of the TV screen, with no sound but the calm narration by the anchors and the sound of sirens from the street. But in that calm, the audience is also watching as about 1,466 people die.

The pain and trauma of September 11 had

People ran for their lives after the towers were hit by planes.

only just begun. Two airplanes had hit the World Trade Center, one the Pentagon, and—though most Americans didn't know it yet—one had flown into a farm field outside of Shanksville, Pennsylvania. That plane was most likely bound for the U.S. Capitol, though no one would ever know for sure. The passengers on board revolted, alarming the hijackers so that they deliberately crashed the plane before it could reach its destination. Thirty-three passengers and seven crew members died protecting their nation.

For the first time in U.S. history, the FAA orders all airborne aircraft to land at the nearest airport. By 12:15 p.m. U.S. airspace is empty of civilian planes and helicopters—approximately 4,500 aircraft have been cleared from the skies. No airplane is to take off again until further notice. The U.S. is shrouded in stunned silence. In just three hours, the path the country is on has changed. And just what the outcome will be, no one yet knows.

***

The terrorist attacks of September 11 unfolded, quite literally, in front of the nation's very eyes. In New York City, all the events except for the first jet hitting the North Tower took place on live television. But unlike many other televised events, no one knew what was happening. No one knew what might happen next. The audience—regular citizens, the president, our military and government, the TV news

> **The terrorist attacks of September 11 unfolded, quite literally, in front of the nation's very eyes.**

Tourists in Times Square watched TV as the events of September 11 unfolded.

reporters, anchors, and producers—were reduced to open-mouthed astonishment. The television producers scrambled to keep up. Reporters were calling in, attacks were happening simultaneously. Buildings were collapsing. People were jumping out of windows to try to escape as there was no other way to leave the building. People were dying.

Television became America's eyes. The cameras kept running. They kept their gaze fixed on the

smoking towers—and then on the rubble—on to
the gaping wound in the Pentagon and eventually,
on the crushed debris in the field in Shanksville,
Pennsylvania. Eventually, the cameras showed
America the survivors covered in white dust, the
firefighters ignoring the risks to their own lives to
save others, and the masses of people searching the
streets for their missing loved ones.

ON THE GROUND ON SEPTEMBER 11

People in the area of the attacks were covered with soot and debris from the falling towers.

On September 11, 2001, Allison Gilbert was a producer for WNBC-TV, the New York area NBC station. She was covering the events near the World Trade Center when the North Tower collapsed:

"I was two blocks from the [North Tower]. I interviewed emergency workers. I looked for my crew and reporter. I grabbed papers full of soot from the ground to see what clues there might be to what had happened and who might have been hurt or killed . . . my back was to the building. I was on the corner of West and Vesey Streets when it started to fall, and I never looked back.

"Everyone around me started running. I started running, trying to outrun a falling skyscraper. I did not know the building was falling straight down. I thought it was going to fall like a tree, smash me into the ground, and kill me. I ran so fast that I ran out of my shoes.

I was barefoot, running over fallen debris, soot, papers, garbage, pieces of concrete and metal. My feet did not feel anything. I just felt fear.

"I saw a concrete barricade of some sort and was trying to get to it for cover when I fell down. My face slammed into the ground. I used my pocketbook to cover my head. Within seconds, I was surrounded by a tornado of thick black smoke and was pelted by debris. I could not see anything, not even my own hands. I could not breathe. I was gasping for air. My mouth was full of so much soot I could bite it. It felt like thick sawdust. It sucked all the moisture out of my mouth.

"I did not know if I was ever going to see the sky again. I was not sure if the building was on top of me, and I was just in an air pocket, or if it had missed me and I was going to live."

ChapterTwo
GAINING UNDERSTANDING: TERRORISM AND THE UNITED STATES

In those very first confusing minutes of September 11, as television stations heard news that a plane had hit the World Trade Center, the baffled anchors and producers did not think of terrorism. Tom Brokaw, the anchor of NBC News in New York City, remembered, "I immediately thought it was probably an accident. It didn't occur to me at that moment that it was terrorism. No one said it was an airliner. I assumed it was a smaller plane." Probably an accident, reporters at news stations thought, and then, when it became clear the plane was a large jet, some thought perhaps a pilot wanted to commit suicide. Once the second plane hit the South Tower, a reporter is heard saying off-camera, "I wonder if there's air traffic control problems."

By 9:18 a.m., 32 minutes after the first plane hit the North Tower, CNN first reported that the plane was hijacked. "AP [Associated Press]: Plane Was Hijacked Before Crashes," a banner at the bottom of the screen read. At 9:30 a.m., President George W. Bush stood at a podium at Emma Booker Elementary School in Sarasota, Florida, and declared, "Two airplanes have crashed into the World Trade Center in an apparent terrorist attack on our country. . . . Terrorism against

"I immediately thought it was probaby an accident. It didn't occur to me at that moment that it was terrorism."

President George W. Bush was visiting an elementary school when he learned of the attack.

our nation will not stand." By 12:00 p.m., CNN carried a banner reading, "America Under Attack." There was no doubt now. What was happening in the country was terrorism.

Nineteen terrorists attacked the United States on September 11. All were men. Fifteen were from Saudi Arabia. Two were from the small Middle Eastern country known as the United Arab Emirates. One terrorist was from Egypt and one from Lebanon.

The three youngest were 20 years old, the oldest 33. The attackers were a part of the radical terrorist group al-Qaida, led by Osama bin Laden. Their goal was to destroy symbolic centers of American finance, military might, and political power. They did this by striking the World Trade Center and the Pentagon. It was believed that they intended to hit the U.S. Capitol had they not been thwarted by the passengers of Flight 93.

Al-Qaida is often called a radical Islamic militant organization. Before the September 11 attacks, it was a controlled operation led by bin Laden, with terrorist groups or cells all over the world, including in Somalia, Egypt, the Philippines, Spain, England, Turkey, and Indonesia. Before September 11 anywhere from 10,000 to 20,000 people—mostly young men—were trained in camps to be al-Qaida workers and attackers. Before bin Laden became involved, the groups of fighters called jihadist cells were often small, weak, and fighting against powerful governments. Bin Laden's eventual goal was to unite these disparate, small groups into one large group, all fighting for the same goal.

In the past, the U.S. had primarily encountered enemies that were part of another country's military. Al-Qaida was a different kind of enemy. Its terrorists struck stealthily, targeted civilians, and did not fight U.S. soldiers on a battlefield, as had enemies in the past. For al-Qaida, the battlefield was literally everywhere and every U.S. man, woman, and child was an enemy soldier to be destroyed.

Osama bin Laden (center) began his terrorist activities in 1990 in Afghanistan.

Al-Qaida described itself as Islamic. However, Muslims around the world and Islamic scholars and clerics stated that al-Qaida does not hold to the principles of the peaceful religion of Islam and does not represent Muslim values, though its members identified themselves as Muslims.

Bin Laden said al-Qaida was waging a war on the U.S., United Kingdom, and Western Europe with the goal of ultimate destruction. At the time of the September 11 attacks, the organization said it had specific demands: It wanted the United States and others to completely leave Saudi Arabia, Iraq,

Afghanistan, and what they call "Palestine"—what many in the world know as Israel and the Palestinian territories. However, some experts believed that even if the U.S. had left these lands, al-Qaida would have continued to terrorize the U.S. and other nations.

Osama bin Laden was the leader of the group. He was a charismatic man who had founded al-Qaida, which means "the base," in 1988. In 1996 and 1998, Bin Laden issued three *fatwas* against the United States. *Fatwas* are rulings on Islamic law given by a cleric or leader. These *fatwas* stated that Muslims must fight violently against Americans all over the world. Al-Qaida would support the terrorist fighters with money, arms, training, and logistics.

In 1998, three years before the September 11 attacks, bin Laden issued a statement titled, "The World Islamic Front for Jihad Against the Jews and Crusaders." The statement declared that America wanted to "annihilate what is left of this people and to humiliate their Muslim neighbors."

Led by bin Laden, al-Qaida bombed American targets. In 1993 investigators suspected that bin Laden organized the planting of a bomb at the World Trade Center—a sign of the destruction that was to follow eight years later. This bomb, planted in a rental truck parked in a garage underneath the building, killed six people and injured more than 1,000. In 1998 bin Laden organized two bombings of the American

WHO WAS OSAMA BIN LADEN?

Osama bin Laden's belief in an anti-Western form of Islam led him to think the U.S. was his enemy.

Osama bin Laden has been called the "North Star" of terrorism. He was the fixed point around which many terrorist groups revolved. But before he was the leader of global terrorism, bin Laden was the 17th of 52 children, born in 1957 to a Yemeni immigrant executive. His father, Muhammad Awad bin Laden, was a billionaire who built mosques and palaces for the Saudi royal family. He was a strict, religious father who insisted that his children work for the family company during the summer. Muhammad had multiple wives—one of them was Osama's mother, a Syrian woman named Hamida al-Attas. He was the only son of that wife.

Most scholars believe that bin Laden led a quiet and deeply religious life when he was young, following an extremely strict anti-Western form of Islam called Wahhabism. Bin Laden never traveled outside the Middle East. He had no associations or friends in the Western world. At King Abdulaziz University in Saudi Arabia, bin Laden began to identify as an Islamic militant. In 1979 he traveled to Afghanistan to help the Islamic fighters who were battling Soviet Union troops. Ironically, U.S. troops were also in Afghanistan, fighting on the same side as bin Laden, against the Soviets. But they did not interact directly with the future leader of terrorism. During his early years in Afghanistan, bin Laden used his family's construction equipment to help build tunnels, shelters, and roads for the Islamic fighters to use.

After 10 years, bin Laden returned to Saudi Arabia. He was a militant fighter and leader now. Bin Laden took over his family's construction business, but he became angry about the Saudi government's close relationship with the U.S. Bin Laden argued that the government should not associate with the Americans. He said that the Americans were arrogant and saw themselves as the leaders of a new world order. Eventually, the Saudi government restricted bin Laden to the city of Jidda (sometimes transliterated as Jeddah). They were afraid that he would offend the U.S. government.

Bin Laden left Saudi Arabia in 1991 and traveled to Sudan. He gathered money and loyal fighters around himself. Bin Laden was ready to begin waging his war against the U.S.

embassies in Kenya and Tanzania. These were also truck bombs, and 224 people were killed. By now, many Americans were familiar with Osama bin Laden, Islamic terrorism, and his goals.

The 19 hijackers chosen for the attack all entered the United States legally, using visas they obtained with their real names. They did not sneak across a border or use false identification. By August 11, one month before the attacks, all 19 were already in the United States. According to ABC News, not only were all the hijackers living in America, bin Laden had also already identified the sites he wanted to strike.

Zacarias Moussaoui

He was just waiting to decide on the exact day the attacks would occur.

Investigators have pieced together some of the hijackers' movements during the weeks before the attacks. Many did ordinary things. Three met in Las Vegas. One hijacker bought a blue jacket at a Florida clothing store. Two others took $2,000 out of an ATM in Florida. A hijacker named Marwan al-Shehhi purchased a one-week gym membership. Investigators know now that Marwan and the other hijackers worked out regularly during their weeks before the attacks.

Another—Zacarias Moussaoui—moved to Minnesota. There, he enrolled at a flight training school. He was learning to be a pilot—but he told his instructors that while he wanted to learn to fly, he did not intend to get a pilot's license. Moussaoui also told them he wanted to learn to fly a big jet—he was thinking of a 747—the type used as commercial airliners, rather than the small planes people often fly for fun. Moussaoui's instructors were alarmed, and contacted the FBI, who began investigating Moussaoui. After a few days, he was arrested.

To carry out the attacks, the hijackers were going to need some flight training. Hani Hanjour was already a pilot—he could fly a plane without radar. But the Saudi Arabian still took about an hour of flight training at an airport in Maryland. Ziad Jarrah asked an instructor at a flight school in Florida to test his piloting skills. At another Florida flight school, Mohammad Atta was training. An instructor remembers hearing him shout, "God is great!" in Arabic while he was in the cockpit. This phrase is sometimes transliterated as "Allahu akabar," which means "God is greater," or "Allahu kabir," which means "God is great." Muslims use this phrase very often in many different situations, but it is also associated with jihadists who are carrying out suicide missions.

On August 20, 22 days before the attack, Hanjour went on the travel website Travelocity. He searched for flights from Washington, D.C., to Los Angeles departing on September 5. Two days later Ziad Jarrah bought a diagram of a 747 cockpit control system and a pilot's GPS. Then, the first plane ticket was bought by a hijacker—Khalid al-Mihdhar—for the date of September 11.

The hijackers all operated openly and legally. They lived in the United States legally. They took flight training legally. They used their email addresses, valid credit cards, and real names to open ticket accounts and buy the airline tickets they used to board the planes legally.

The federal government did know that some of the hijackers were in the United States. The government was conducting general investigations into bin Laden's terrorist network in the United

The hijackers all operated openly and legally. They lived in the United States legally.

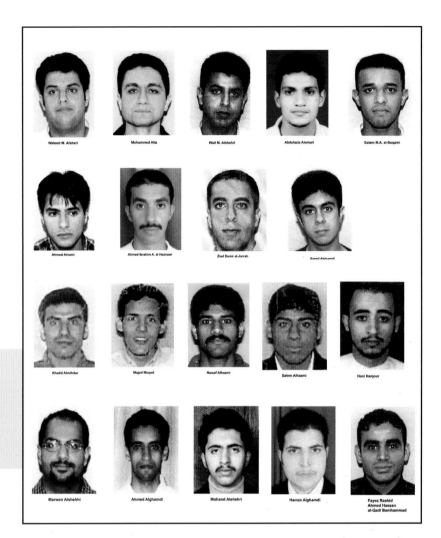

This FBI poster shows the 19 hijackers suspected in the three 9/11 attacks.

States. On August 27, for instance, the Immigration and Naturalization Service revoked the visa of one of the hijackers. On August 15 government terrorism experts warned those in the executive branch of the possibility of a terrorist attack on American soil. But there was little sense of urgency. No one thought an attack was so close.

On August 23 the attackers had a final planning meeting at the Valencia Motel in Laurel, Maryland. Mohammad Atta led the meeting. Plans continued to go forward. Another hijacker, Nawaf al-Hazmi, bought a folding pocket knife at Target. One by one, the hijackers bought their plane tickets. Mohammad Atta bought a knife. Waleed al-Shehri bought a shirt and a pair of khakis. They had neat haircuts, trimmed facial hair, or clean-shaven faces, and tidy, ordinary Western clothing.

On September 6 bin Laden was told that the attacks were scheduled for September 11. Two of the hijackers flew from Florida to Boston. Others flew to Newark, New Jersey. They emptied their bank accounts and wired the money home. They went out to dinner.

September 11. Morning. Mohammad Atta and fellow hijacker Abdul Aziz al Omari flew to Boston from Portland, Maine. They passed through security in Portland without incident and boarded American Airlines Flight 11, flying from Logan International Airport in Boston to Los Angeles. In video from a security camera, Atta and al Omari are seen at the security gate, neatly dressed in sport shirts and slacks, holding carry-on bags, with their tickets in their hands. Atta's bag contained a knife and Mace.

Out on the tarmac, two pieces of luggage labeled M. Atta arrived after the cargo doors were closed. Workers put the luggage on the next flight to Los Angeles. The flight took off at 7:59 a.m.

In Washington, D.C.'s, Dulles Airport, hijackers

Salem and Nawaf al-Hazmi set off the alarms twice at security but were cleared the third time.

Salem al-Hazmi and Nawaf al-Hazmi can be seen in a security camera image at the security gate. They both wear tidy, collared sports shirts and pants. They look like business travelers. One has a bulky black carry-on bag over his shoulder. One is carrying an object in his back pocket.

The hijackers were carrying small metal knives and box cutters. These items should have set off the security gate, and three did. Screeners tested them again. Two of the three passed this time—even though they still had their knives and box cutters. The third hijacker set off the alarm a second time.

A screener passed a hand-wand over him. He was cleared. The hijackers boarded American Airlines Flight 77 from Dulles to Los Angeles. The flight took off at 8:21 a.m.

Less is known about the movements of the hijackers before they boarded Flight 175 from Logan Airport in Boston to Los Angeles and Flight 93 from Newark, New Jersey, to San Francisco.

Over the days and weeks and months that followed September 11, investigators pieced together some of the story of what happened during the flights themselves. They researched the hijackers and discovered how they entered the country and what they did to prepare for the attack. And in reports, it became clear that the government was aware multiple times that a terrorist strike from al-Qaida could happen. The government did not realize, though, just how soon and when and where it would occur.

ChapterThree
WATCHING LIVE

The second plane changed what people perceived on September 11. Before 9:02 a.m. the news anchors and reporters still thought the strike on the North Tower might have been an accident. "Was this purely an accident or could this have been an intentional act?" NBC anchor Lauer asked at 9:00 a.m.

Jon Scott was anchoring Fox News in New York City that morning. He remembered, "I asked [a commercial airline accident expert] how a pilot could have made such a catastrophic mistake. . . . As I spoke . . . my eyes were glued to the live helicopter feed. . . . Something caught my eye—something moving in the lower right-hand corner of the monitor."

At 9:02 a.m., reporters and pilots from various networks were hovering in helicopters near the smoking North Tower. Their cameras were fixed on the tower, which stood out silver and black against the deep blue sky. John del Giorno, a helicopter reporter for the New York ABC affiliate, WABC-TV, was in the air filming. In 2002 he recalled, "We were climbing through 1,100 feet . . . and then we saw it. Paul Smith, my pilot, saw it before I did—an airliner, traveling from south to north, traveling low and fast . . . it flew into the shade being created by the smoke plume from the North Tower. Something made me reach for the

remote that controls our onboard tape deck and point
our camera at the World Trade Center. I moved and
focused the camera, placed the remote in my lap,
pressed 'play' and 'record,' and looked back at my
camera monitor. It now contained the image of a
huge fireball."

On TV screens, Flight 175 flew into the corner of
the screen and disappeared. It was inside the South
Tower now. A second later, a huge red, black, and

yellow fireball erupted from within the top third of the South Tower. Billows of black smoke competed with the smoke pouring from the North Tower. Below the fireball, a shower of debris and fire rained down—paper, metal shards, and the pulverized pieces of the plane and building.

For people watching on TV, two things happened in that moment. The first was that, because of the delay in communications, for a few seconds the audience saw the second plane before the anchors did. Couric was still talking about emergency vehicles when the audience saw the plane enter the corner of the camera frame and move toward the South Tower. Even the cameraman had cut from a wide shot of the towers to a close-up of the top of the North Tower. The audience saw something that no one else had yet—not the producer on the ground who was speaking with Couric, not the cameraman in the helicopter. For 3 seconds, there was no interpretation or filter between the audience and the events. The TV camera was simply eyes—seeing and recording. For a few seconds, the TV audience was in charge of its own interpretation. And as the reaction from the reporters and newsrooms began, in that moment, the professionals were also simply viewers. The sense of authority and interpretation that the newsroom provided had momentarily disappeared.

Then, in the space of a few more seconds, the

Hovering helicopters filmed the damage caused by the planes.

producer saw the impact, the anchor reacted, and the camera pulled back to reveal the wide shot of the second tower with the fireball exploding out of its side. In that moment, what the eyes saw changed. When the audience looked at the TV screen before that moment, it saw possibly a terrorist act or possibly an accident. Then, with the impact of the second plane, those possibilities were wiped out. It was undoubtedly a terrorist attack.

At the time, Peter Jennings was the national anchor of ABC News. He died in 2005. But in 2002, he

People on the
ground after the
attacks were scared
but relieved to be
safe and alive.

remembered, "I simply put my hands in the air and told everybody in the newsroom to stay quiet, because we didn't know what was happening. . . . Rather than risk saying something foolish, I let the audience absorb it." In that moment, the TV's support system— the anchors, the reporters, the crew—stepped aside. They left the audience alone with the camera. The audience and the professionals were all together, on the same level—simply witnesses and nothing more.

The change in TV coverage on September 11 reflected the magnitude of what was happening to the country. The planes in Washington, D.C., and New York City had not only hit the financial and political capitals of the United States—they had also hit the media centers. Massive media infrastructure was already in place in those cities—newsrooms, antennas, helicopters, reporters on the ground. This system was able to mobilize very quickly to allow images to be immediately broadcast. CNN and other news channels switched over from their regular programming to significant breaking news. Significant breaking news is different from both breaking news and live news. All airtime was given over to the events in New York, Washington, D.C., and Pennsylvania. There were no commercial breaks. The coverage was measured in hours and days, rather than in minutes, as news coverage is normally measured.

There had been other significant breaking news stories. When President John F. Kennedy was assassinated in November 1963 the networks stayed with the story for four days. The actual shooting wasn't covered live on TV, but the networks covered everything else without commercials. Coverage went on, depending on the network, between 55 and 71 hours. It included the assassination of Lee Harvey Oswald, the suspected shooter, by Jack Ruby. In 1991 CNN reporters broadcast live audio footage of the bombs falling on Baghdad, marking the start of the

The coverage was measured in hours and days, rather than in minutes . . .

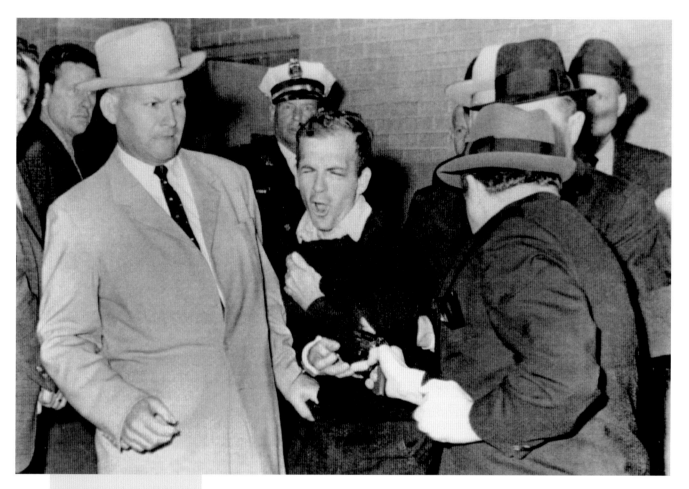

When Jack Ruby shot Lee Harvey Oswald, it was captured in real time by TV cameras.

first U.S. airstrikes in Iraq. The year 1995 showed the bombing of the Oklahoma City federal building on TV. But September 11 marked the first time TV viewers saw the nation attacked in real time.

On September 11 news stations also began using the "ticker"—a steady stream of headlines and news bites that runs continually along the bottom of the screen while the programming goes on. News was overwhelming on the day of the attacks. Stations had to report on multiple events happening at the same time. Putting some of the news on a ticker allowed the stations to report as much as possible. The news ticker had been used before—for national emergencies, election results, or extreme weather. But it always disappeared once the event was over. After September 11 the news ticker stayed and can still be seen crawling at the bottom of the screen on many news shows.

After the strikes, many journalists and private citizens began filming street-level shots. These videos were offered to TV stations and edited together. By September 12 images were being broadcast of the collapse of the South Tower from a street view. As the building disintegrated, a massive gray dust cloud billowed up and rolled down the street like a tidal wave as people ran toward the camera, away from the cloud. Later, shaky footage shows streets coated with so much white dust it looks like snow. Office paper is everywhere, coating the ground as well. Dazed people in business clothes, covered in dust, sit in rows on edges and curbs. EMTs, ignoring the cameras, give each other orders, loading objects in and out of ambulances. People hold up other people. People cry as they talk.

The wail of fire engines was one of the first sounds people heard after the North Tower strike. Battalion Chief Joseph Pfeifer ordered engine and ladder companies, fire chiefs, and specialized units to the scene of the strike. Police and paramedics

Firefighters, journalists, and New Yorkers who had lost loved ones were among those at the site.

were ordered in by emergency dispatchers. The September 11 response had begun. In the end, 214 fire units with 112 engines, 58 ladder trucks, five rescue companies, and dozens more vehicles and squads, along with 2,000 police officers, would risk their lives to save as many people as they could on that day.

But the responders were also victims. Many, particularly firefighters, were killed themselves. Some were hit by falling debris. Many were trapped inside the towers when they collapsed. During the immediate response period, 343 firefighters and paramedics were killed, along with 60 police officers.

Rehema Ellis was a correspondent for NBC News. After the North Tower collapsed, she walked as close as she could get to the site. "People were standing around just looking dazed," she later wrote. "There was paper from the tower collapse still flying in the air, swirling around. People were picking up pieces that looked like treasure maps, the edges charred and frayed."

Viewers of the live coverage briefly saw the most disturbing images from 9/11. Many people trapped in the burning towers jumped from windows to their deaths as the towers burned around them. They jumped, fell, and struck the ground in full view of people standing and watching. CNN briefly aired this footage live before those in the newsroom registered what the camera was recording. Then CNN made the decision not to replay this footage at all. Camera operators were on the ground at this point, and they shot video of the people jumping. "It was the hardest and saddest video I have ever shot," Fox News cameraman Robert Ginnane said later. "I saw about 15 people jump to their deaths. I [took] shot[s] of two of these jumpers and then I turned my camera off. I was overcome."

The World Trade Center was the most dramatic strike of the day, but it was not the only one. Hani Hanjour crashed Flight 77 from Dulles Airport into

"It was the hardest and saddest video I have ever shot."

INSIDE THE TOWER

Survivors of the attack made their way through the nearby streets to safety.

Brian Clark was one of the few people who escaped the South Tower above the level where the plane hit. On September 11 he was at his job as a vice president at a company called Euro Brokers. In September 2016 Clark gave an interview to the *Here & Now* public radio show on Boston's WBUR. He recalls what happened at the moment the plane struck, and immediately afterward.

"Our floor just fell apart. Everything came out of the ceiling—air conditioning ducts and speakers, the works, if you like, fell down. No electricity. The air was filled with white, chalky construction dust. There was no flames, no smoke at that point. And the building swayed—for 10 seconds I was terrified—and fortunately, for me, in hindsight, that was the only moment of the day that I was afraid. . . . Whether this really happened or not,

I can't say with certainty, but the sensation was . . . the building swayed six to eight feet. And then it stopped. And then for five seconds it came back to vertical. . .

"I started down Stairway A. . . . And with the six or eight people following me down the stairs in the darkness with my flashlight on, we only went down three floors. . . . I was distracted . . . by a stranger's voice inside the 81st floor. . . . I continued on to this stranger, kind of dug him out of the rubble and the two of us went back to the stairway. And I guess that was the fateful moment: I shined the light down the stairs. I only saw smoke billowing up, not any flames and we just started down. We dug our way through a lot of rubble, and got out of the building at about 4 minutes to 10."

The South Tower collapsed at 9:59 a.m.

the Pentagon in Arlington, Virginia, just before 9:38 a.m. The crash demolished a section of the huge five-sided building and killed everyone on the plane and 125 people inside. The plane flew into the building so low that it clipped the top of lampposts on the sidewalks. A pilot who watched the plane go into the Pentagon reported that the pilot—whom we now know was Hanjour—added power as he approached the building.

There was no live TV footage of the plane plowing into the Pentagon as there was of the second plane hitting the South Tower and the collapse of both towers in New York. Anchors were still focused on the events in New York City. On NBC it was not until 9:41 a.m., 3 minutes after the strike, that the screen finally showed a hazy helicopter's-eye view of the smoking, low building.

Later, viewers saw many shots of the caved-in, blackened section of the building. But unlike the strikes on the Twin Towers, which were portrayed as separate headline events, the strike on the Pentagon was folded more into the overall narrative. It was just one more event in a day full of events. But the strike did shift the TV story of that day. If the second strike on the towers changed the narrative from a possible accident to an act of terror, then, Jennings of ABC recalled a few years before his death, "When the Pentagon was hit in Washington, it became pretty clear we had an act of war."

This aerial view shows the Pentagon after it was attacked.

During the first hours of the TV coverage that day, the cameras showed only long shots of the towers—and then dust clouds after the collapse. Away from the immediate destruction, TV cameras were able to film some of the response: dozens of smoke- and dust-covered firefighters and paramedics giving water and treatment to dazed survivors sitting on curbs and benches. By early afternoon NBC managed to interview eyewitnesses, including first responders. A firefighter covered in soot tells the reporter that he spent a year in combat and never saw anything

like this. His voice breaks and he folds his lips and shakes his head as he tries to knock some of the debris out of his jacket. A police officer tells the reporter that they simply carried dead bodies away that they found lying in the debris. The camera shows shots of massed police officers wearing face masks as they prepare to enter the destruction zone. Off-camera correspondent Ellis frantically reports on the crowding of the hospitals with survivors.

There was one more image the TV cameras showed that day, and it wasn't broadcast until hours after the other images. This image is different from the others. This is an image of what didn't happen.

Flight 93 was hijacked by Ziad Jarrah and three others. Most likely, they meant to fly it into the U.S. Capitol, investigators have determined. But they were prevented from doing so when a group of passengers decided to revolt. They attempted to break into the locked cockpit as the hijackers were at the controls. By placing secret phone calls, these passengers and others on the plane had learned of the other hijackings. They realized that the hijackers meant to fly the plane into a building, killing all onboard and most likely hundreds or thousands on the ground.

The passengers decided they would not let that happen.

These passengers banded together and tried to storm the cockpit, possibly by ramming a service cart into the door. Inside, the hijackers realized what was happening. They deliberately aborted their original plan and purposely crashed the plane upside down at 563 miles per hour (906 km/hr) into a field in Pennsylvania. Everyone on board died instantly.

TV's story of Flight 93 was a quieter one. It was not captured live and in-depth, as were the events in New York and Washington, D.C. No media infrastructure existed in the remote area to support this kind of reporting, as it did in the cities. The pictures that were shown were after the event and were not dramatic—fire engines parked in an empty

Investigators
searched the crash
site of Flight 93
looking for debris
and evidence.

field, surrounded by woods. Firefighters in their gear
striding around unhurriedly. There were no survivors.
Just a crater in the rocky soil and piles of scorched,
blackened earth. As the story of September 11 took
shape in TV newsrooms, the cameras showed a
continuous loop of the video from the Twin Towers
strike and the aftermath. Sometimes, they cut to the
Pentagon. But only rarely did the newsroom feed
show the field in Pennsylvania. Only later did the
story of the passengers' bravery begin to emerge.

ChapterFour
HISTORY CHANGED FOREVER

At 8:30 p.m. on September 11 President George W. Bush addressed the country on live television. All of the networks and cable news channels carried his speech. He sat at his desk in the Oval Office, composed, hands folded in front of him. He said, "The pictures of airplanes flying into buildings, fires burning, huge structures collapsing, have filled us with disbelief, terrible sadness, and a quiet, unyielding anger. These acts of mass murder were intended to frighten our nation into chaos and retreat. But they have failed; our country is strong. A great people has been moved to protect a great nation. Terrorist attacks can shake the foundations of our biggest buildings, but they cannot touch the foundation of America. These acts shattered steel, but they cannot dent the steel of American resolve."

The impact of September 11 was immediate and lasting. The events were broadcast live, as they happened. All of America felt intimately involved. And September 11 changed the country's future, reshaping the way we thought of terrorism.

Thousands of firefighters, police officers, rescue dogs, Red Cross workers, construction workers, and civilian volunteers began a clean-up effort that was to last 8 months and 19 days. Eventually 1.8 million tons

of rubble would be removed from the site. The site of
the destroyed World Trade Center quickly became
known as Ground Zero and the images broadcast
from there became symbols of the United States'
struggle to heal.

The television continued to be both the nation's
eyes on the tragedy and the medium that shaped the
narrative. By September 15 commercials had resumed
on many networks, but the programming continued
to be almost entirely focused on the events of
September 11. The camera showed shots of massive,

LASTING HEALTH PROBLEMS OF FIRST RESPONDERS AND SURVIVORS

Firefighters were among the first responders. Later, many suffered serious health problems as a result.

In New York City, between 60,000 to 70,000 firefighters, police officers, construction workers, and volunteers remained at Ground Zero for days and weeks after all the survivors had left. Hundreds of others worked at the sites at the Pentagon and in Pennsylvania. Sifting through the mountains of ash and debris, the first responders and workers also breathed in fine dust made of a dangerous mixture of glass, aluminum, asbestos, and burned up jet fuel.

In the 16 years since September 11 doctors realized that this mixture has caused serious, lasting health problems for those who breathed it. People who worked at Ground Zero, and also those who simply lived near it, are at a higher risk of breathing problems, such as asthma, and prostate and thyroid cancer, as well as other problems, including post-traumatic stress disorder and back pain.

staggering piles of rubble. The twisted masses looked impossible to clean up, but the cameras also showed construction equipment slowly moving through the terrain that now looked like a war zone. Viewers saw streets so coated with white ash that they looked like an unpainted stage set.

And in addition to simply broadcasting the images, TV began to function as a place for people to deposit their thoughts, memories, and emotions. Quickly, TV stations put together shows focused around September 11. The coverage shifted from the actual events of the day to recovery and tracking

. . . 80 million people watched TV coverage of September 11 on the evening of the attacks . . .

those responsible. A special called *Asking, Listening, Healing* was broadcast on NBC's New York City station on September 15. With soft introductory music and hazy shots of people lighting memorial candles, the TV hosts coordinated discussions with therapists, parents, and high school students wearing big name tags. Public service announcements for grief counseling and donation drop-offs punctuated the program. A nationally broadcast tribute concert and fundraiser aired on December 4. Comedy hosts including David Letterman and Jay Leno and comedy shows such as *Saturday Night Live* struggled with how to address the tragedy. The media and the public were figuring out together how to talk about this narrative.

Afterward, Nielsen Media Research reported that 80 million people watched TV coverage of September 11 on the evening of the attacks—about the same number as watch the Super Bowl each year. A Pew Research survey reported that 89 percent of Americans felt positive about the news media coverage of the tragic event.

September 11 led to war. Less than one month later, on October 7, U.S. and British air strikes began in Afghanistan, hitting targets associated with al-Qaida and with the Taliban, the group accused of sheltering al-Qaida. By October 19 U.S. ground troops were operating in Afghanistan in what the

After the attacks, the focus shifted to looking for those who were lost in the destruction.

White House called Operation Enduring Freedom. A second war in Iraq was started by the United States in 2003. The war in Afghanistan would go on for 13 years, until December 28, 2014, when President Barack Obama declared the war officially over. But thousands of U.S. soldiers remain in Afghanistan to this day, as part of efforts that began because of September 11. The war succeeded in destroying the Taliban and in supporting the Afghan people and

Several ships were sent to aid Operation Enduring Freedom in Afghanistan.

their government against the Taliban. But by 2017, 2,403 U.S. soldiers had died and the cost to the U.S. was estimated to be as high as $2 trillion.

TV continued to play a role in the remembrance of September 11. On the first anniversary, networks showed special, all-day coverage of the ceremonies taking place at Ground Zero and the Pentagon. They also broadcast documentaries, compilations of professional and amateur video, and replays of Bush's addresses to the nation. The annual ceremonies have continued to be televised in the years since.

In 2006 construction began on an important step in the healing story of September 11—the creation of a memorial at the site of the World Trade Center. For five years, curators and historians painfully, painstakingly collected artifacts, recorded stories, and gathered names of survivors and victims. Two pools of water are left in the footprints of the Twin Towers, with a walkway of more than 400 trees leading up to the pools. The memorial opened to the public in 2011. In 2008 a memorial was unveiled at the Pentagon, and in 2015, a memorial to Flight 93 was opened to the public on the site of the Pennsylvania crash.

Another important milestone was reached when Osama bin Laden was found and killed at his compound in Pakistan by U.S. Navy SEALs on May 2, 2011, Pakistan time. Obama and his cabinet and advisers watched on a live camera as the soldiers broke into the compound and shot bin Laden. Just after midnight Eastern Time on May 1 the president announced the victory to the U.S.

On September 11 television showed us the story of both the visible and the invisible. Some parts of September 11 were horribly, painfully visible: the towers collapsing on live television, the street-level video footage shot by bystanders and shown on

TV, the bleeding, dust-covered, stunned people, the firefighters crying on camera. These parts of the story were almost *more* visible—more raw, more unfiltered, and unedited—than usual.

Then there were the parts of the story we did not see—the invisible parts. Watching the towers collapse, we did not see the thousands of people dying inside at that moment. The story of Flight 93 was invisible, until much, much later, when investigators pieced together what happened. The struggles on the planes were invisible, captured only

by fragments of phone calls and audio recordings. The videos of people jumping from the buildings were shown live once, but never again. Those images have become invisible now too.

Making stories out of events helps us to understand what has happened and why. The very next day, September 12, CNN carried the constant banner on its screen of "America Under Attack." That was the title of the story. Reading that title flavored how we saw what CNN showed us.

As the days and weeks—and years—wore on, the pieces of the story of September 11 slotted into place. Television's gaze helped create this story for us. The raw live coverage of that day seared the trauma into the American mind. The television became our eyes. And later, it became our storyteller. We needed to shape the events of that day into a narrative. Otherwise, we could not heal or move on. TV creates stories. And the events of September 11 eventually became a story too—a story about America, its people, and its place in the world.

Timeline

January 15, 2000

The first two September 11 hijackers enter the United States on legal visas. By June 29, 2001, all 19 hijackers are in the United States

August 27, 2001

Leader Mohammad Atta holds a final planning meeting with the rest of the Flight 77 hijackers at the Valencia Motel in Laurel, Maryland

September 11, 2001, 7:59 a.m.

Flight 11 takes off from Boston bound for Los Angeles, with 11 crew, 76 passengers, and 5 hijackers on board

September 11, 2001, 8:14 a.m.

Flight 175 takes off from Boston bound for Los Angeles, with 9 crew, 51 passengers, and 5 hijackers

September 11, 2001, 8:49 a.m.

For more than 72 hours, the longest period in television history, the three major networks—ABC, NBC, and CBS—broadcast news exclusively related to one event—the attacks, without commercials. CNN is the first TV network to cut into regular programming, broadcasting images of the smoking North Tower

September 11, 2001, 9:03 a.m.

Piloted by Marwan al-Shehhi, Flight 175 crashes into the South Tower of the World Trade Center through floors 77 to 85. All onboard the flight and an unknown number of people inside are killed

September 11, 2001, 9:30 a.m.

President George W. Bush addresses the country from Sarasota, Florida, and refers to the events as a terrorist attack

September 11, 2001, 8:20 a.m.

Flight 77 takes off from Washington, D.C., bound for Los Angeles, with 6 crew, 53 passengers, and five hijackers on board

September 11, 2001, 8:42 a.m.

Flight 93 takes off from Newark, New Jersey, bound for San Francisco, with 7 crew, 33 passengers, and 4 hijackers

September 11, 2001, 8:46 a.m.

Piloted by Mohammad Atta, Flight 11 crashes into the North Tower of the World Trade Center between floors 93 and 99. All on board the plane and hundreds inside are killed instantly

September 11, 2001, 9:37 a.m.

Flight 77 crashes into the Pentagon, killing all on the plane and 125 people on the ground. Hani Hanjour is the pilot

September 11, 2001, 9:45 a.m.

For the first time in U.S. aviation history, the Federal Aviation Administration orders all planes in the United States to land at the nearest airport. By about 12:15 p.m., U.S. airspace is clear of all civilian aircraft. The airspace is closed

Timeline

September 11, 2001, 9:59 a.m.

The South Tower collapses in 10 seconds on live TV, killing 624 people or more in the building and on the ground

September 11, 2001, 10:03 a.m.

Hijacker pilot Ziad Jarrah crashes Flight 93 into a Pennsylvania field after passengers attempt to storm the cockpit. All on board are killed

September 11, 2001, 10:28 a.m.

The North Tower collapses on live TV, bringing the death toll to 1,466 people

October 7, 2001

U.S. air strikes begin in Afghanistan, as retaliation for the September 11 attacks

May 30, 2002

Clean up is officially ended at Ground Zero, after 3.1 million people-hours of labor

September 11, 2008

The National 9/11 Pentagon Memorial in Arlington County, Virginia, is opened to the public

May 1, 2011

Osama bin Laden is killed by U.S. Navy SEALs at his compound in Pakistan

September 11, 2001, 8:30 p.m.

President George W. Bush addresses the nation from the White House

September 11, 2001

Recovery and clean-up begin at Ground Zero. Thousands of workers labor around the clock to remove 1.8 million tons of rubble

September 11, 2011

The National September 11 Memorial and Museum, dedicated to the victims' families, opens to the public on the site of the World Trade Center on September 12

December 28, 2014

The U.S. officially ends its combat operations in Afghanistan. The active military presence in Afghanistan will continue for several more years

September 10, 2015

A permanent memorial, the Flight 93 Memorial Center, is opened in Somerset County, Pennsylvania

Glossary

abort—bring to a premature end because of a problem

anchor—person who presents and coordinates a live television show

aviation—the operation or flying of aircraft

disparate—essentially different, cannot be compared

embassy—the official residence or office of an ambassador

hijacker—a person who illegally takes control of a vehicle, such as an aircraft, ship or car, and forces it to go to a different destination or uses it for his or her own purposes

interpretation—the action of explaining the meaning of something

jihadist—a person involved in a struggle or fight against Islam

radical—promoting or based on complete social or political change

surreptitious—secret

terrorism—the unlawful use of violence, especially against civilians, in pursuit of political change

visa—a stamp on a passport indicating that the holder of the passport may legally enter, leave and stay in a country for a specific period of time

Wahhabism—a strict, austere form of Islam that insists on a literal interpretation of the Koran, the Islamic holy book

Additional Resources

Further Reading

Brown, Don. *America Is Under Attack: September 11, 2001*. New York: Square Fish, 2014.

Gassman, Julie. *Saved by the Boats: The Heroic Sea Evacuation of September 11*. Mankato, MN: Capstone, 2016.

Nardo, Don. *Ground Zero: How a Photograph Sent a Message of Hope*. Mankato, MN: Capstone, 2016.

Zullo, Allan. *10 True Tales: Heroes of 9/11*. New York: Scholastic, 2015.

Internet Sites

Use FactHound to find Internet sites related to this book.
Visit *www.facthound.com*
Just type in 9780756558338 and go.

Critical Thinking Questions

Major unexpected events were shown live on television on September 11. How does seeing an event live on TV compare with seeing an event taped and broadcast later? Name three differences.

The text makes the point that the TV networks were able to shape the September 11 coverage by choosing the images they showed over and over. Identify the basic story they told. Now, tell the story from a different global perspective. What are the differences in the new story? What are the similarities?

Many camera operators and television producers made the decision not to air video of people falling and jumping from the World Trade Center. Do you agree or disagree with this decision? Give your reasons.

Source Notes

All broadcast times given in Chapters 1-4 are drawn from "Understanding September 11: Television New Archive." Internet Archive: The Understanding 9/11 TV News Collection, https://archive.org/details/911 Accessed September 18, 2017

p. 7, "We can only hope the area has been evacuated..." Erik Lipton. "Study Maps the Location of Deaths in the Twin Towers." *New York Times*, July 22, 2004, http://www.nytimes.com/2004/07/22/nyregion/study-maps-the-location-of-deaths-in-the-twin-towers.html Accessed December 13, 2017

p. 8, "...apparent terrorist attack..." George W. Bush. "Remarks on the Terrorist Attack on New York City's World Trade Center in Sarasota, Florida" (speech, Sarasota, Florida, September 11, 2001), U.S. Government Publishing Office, https://www.gpo.gov/fdsys/pkg/WCPD-2001-09-17/html/WCPD-2001-09-17-Pg1300.htm Accessed September 18, 2017

p. 13, "I was two blocks from the [North Tower]..." Allison Gilbert, Phil Hirschkorn, Melinda Murphy, Robyn Walensky, and Mitchell Stephens, eds. *Covering Catastrophe: Broadcast Journalists Report September 11*. Chicago: Bonus Books, 2002, pp. 124-129.

p. 14, "I wonder if there's air traffic control problems..." "Understanding September 11."

p. 14, "Two airplanes have crashed into the World Trade Center in an apparent terrorist attack on our country..." "Remarks by the President George W. Bush After Two Planes Crash into World Trade Center."

p. 27, "I asked [a commercial airline accident expert] how a pilot could have made such a catastrophic mistake..." *Covering Catastrophe: Broadcast Journalists Report September 11,* p. 28.

p. 27, "We were climbing through 1,100 feet ..." *Covering Catastrophe: Broadcast Journalists Report September 11,* p. 30.

p. 31, "I simply put my hands in the air..." *Covering Catastrophe: Broadcast Journalists Report September 11,* p. 34.

p. 36, "People were standing around just looking dazed..." *Covering Catastrophe: Broadcast Journalists Report September 11,* p. 115

p. 36, "It was the hardest and saddest video I have ever shot..." *Covering Catastrophe: Broadcast Journalists Report September 11,* p. 53

p. 38, "When the Pentagon was hit in Washington..." Allison Gilbert, Phil Hirschkorn, Melinda Murphy, Robyn Walensky, and Mitchell Stephens, eds. *Covering Catastrophe: Broadcast Journalists Report September 11,* p. 73

p. 43, "The pictures of airplanes flying into buildings..." "Remarks by the President George W. Bush After Two Planes Crash into World Trade Center."

Select Bibliography

"11 September 2001 Hijackers." Central Intelligence Agency, June 18,. 2002, https://www.cia.gov/news-information/speeches-testimony/2002/DCI_18_June_testimony_new.pdf

"1993 World Trade Center Bombing Fast Facts." CNN Library, Feb. 21, 2017, http://www.cnn.com/2013/11/05/us/1993-world-trade-center-bombing-fast-facts/index.html

"9/11 Survivor Brian Clark Reflects on His Escape, 15 Years Later." *WBUR: Here & Now*, Sept. 7, 2016, http://www.wbur.org/hereandnow/2016/09/07/911-survivor-brian-clark

"A Biography of Osama bin Laden." *PBS: Frontline*, Nov. 8, 2017. https://www.pbs.org/wgbh/pages/frontline/shows/binladen/who/bio.html

"American Psyche Reeling From Terror Attacks." Pew Research Center, Sept. 19, 2001, . http://www.people-press.org/2001/09/19/american-psyche-reeling-from-terror-attacks/

Byman, Daniel L. "Comparing Al Qaeda and ISIS: Different Goals, Different Targets: Testimony." Brookings Institute, Apr. 29, 2015, https://www.brookings.edu/testimonies/comparing-al-Qaida-and-isis-different-goals-different-targets/

Calhoun, Craig, Paul Price, and Ashley Timmer, eds. *Understanding September 11.* New York: The New Press, 2002.

Carter, Bill, and Jim Rutenberg. "After the Attacks: Television; Viewers Again Return to Traditional Networks." *New York Times*, Sept. 15, 2001, http://www.nytimes.com/2001/09/15/us/after-the-attacks-television-viewers-again-return-to-traditional-networks.html?pagewanted=print

"Ceremony closes 'Ground Zero' cleanup." CNN.com, May 30, 2002, http://edition.cnn.com/2002/US/05/30/rec.wtc.cleanup/

Conant, Eve. "Terror: The Remains of the 9/11 Hijackers." *Newsweek*, Jan. 2, 2009, http://www.newsweek.com/terror-remains-911-hijackers-78327

Dudziak, Mary, ed. *September 11 in History: A Watershed Moment?* Durham, NC: Duke University Press, 2003.

"FBI Announces List of 19 Hijackes." Federal Bureau of Investigation National Press Office. Sept. 14, 2001, https://archives.fbi.gov/archives/news/pressrel/press-releases/fbi-announces-list-of-19-hijackers

"Flight 93 hijacker: 'Shall we finish it off?' 9/11 report reveals who was at controls before crash." CNN.com, July 23, 2004, http://www.cnn.com/2004/US/07/22/911.flight.93/index.html

Gilbert, Allison, Phil Hirschkorn, Melinda Murphy, Robyn Walensky, and Mitchell Stephens, eds. *Covering Catastrophe: Broadcast Journalists Report September 11.* Chicago: Bonus Books, 2002.

Glaberson, William. "After the Attacks: United Flight 175; Second Plane to Strike World Trade Center Tower Took a Deliberate Path." *New York Times.* Sept. 13, 2001, http://www.nytimes.com/2001/09/13/us/after-attacks-united-flight-175-second-plane-strike-world-trade-center-tower.html

Hansen, Matt. "9/11 Responders who became ill from toxic exposure now have a monument to their heroism." *Los Angeles Times*, Sept. 10, 2017, http://beta.latimes.com/nation/la-na-new-york-9-11-responders-20170910-story.html

"History and Culture: The Flight 93 Story." National Park Service Flight 93 National Memorial, Sept. 19, 2017, https://www.nps.gov/flni/learn/historyculture/index.htm

"How 9-11 Changed the Evening News." Pew Research Center: Journalism and Media, Sept. 11, 2006, http://www.journalism.org/2006/09/11/how-9-11-changed-the-evening-news/

"Jihad Against Jews and Crusaders: World Islamic Front Statement." Federation of American Scientists. October 2017. https://fas.org/irp/world/para/docs/980223-fatwa.htm

Leopold, Todd. "The making of a memorial: Reshaping ground zero." CNN, Sept. 1, 2011, http://www.cnn.com/2011/US/08/31/911.memorial/index.html

Life: One Nation: America Remembers September 11, 2001: 10 Years Later. New York: Little, Brown and Co., 2011.

Lipton, Erik. "Study Maps the Location of Deaths in the Twin Towers." *New York Times*, July 22, 2004, http://www.nytimes.com/2004/07/22/nyregion/study-maps-the-location-of-deaths-in-the-twin-towers.html

Moore, John. "The Evolution of Islamic Terrorism: An Overview." *PBS: Frontline*, Sept. 25, 2017, https://www.pbs.org/wgbh/pages/frontline/shows/target/etc/modern.html

"Osama bin Laden Fast Facts." CNN Library, June 6, 2017, http://www.cnn.com/2013/08/30/world/osama-bin-laden-fast-facts/index.html

"Remarks by the President George W. Bush After Two Planes Crash into World Trade Center." 9/11 Memorial and Museum. 11 Sept. 2001. 10 Oct. 2017. https://www.911memorial.org/sites/default/files/Remarks%20by%20President%20Bush%20After%20Two%20Planes%20Crash%20Into%20World%20Trade%20Center.pdf

Reynolds, Amy and Brooke Barnett. "America Under Attack": CNN's Verbal and Visual Framing of September 11. *Media Representations of September 11.* Steven Chermak, Frankie Y. Bailey, and Michelle Brown, eds. Westport, CT: Praeger, 2003. P. 85-102.

Ross, Brian. "While America Slept: The True Story of 9/11." ABC New, Nov. 16, 2017, http://abcnews.go.com/Blotter/ten-years-ago-today-countdown-911/story?id=14191671

"September 11 Attack Timeline." 9/11 Memorial and Museum, Sept. 26, 2017, http://timeline.911memorial.org/#Timeline/2

"September 11: Bearing Witness to History." Smithsonian National Museum of American History, Sept. 22, 2017, http://amhistory.si.edu/september11/

"The World Trade Center History." 9/11 Memorial and Museum, Oct. 7, 2017, https://www.911memorial.org/world-trade-center-history

"Timeline for American Airlines Flight 77." NPR. 17 Jun. 2004, Nov. 28, 2017, https://www.npr.org/templates/story/story.php?storyId=1962742

"Timeline for United Airlines Flight 175." National Public Radio, June 17, 2004, https://www.npr.org/templates/story/story.php?storyId=1962517

"Understanding September 11: A Television News Archive." Internet Archive: The Understanding 9/11 TV News Collection, Sept. 18, 2017, https://archive.org/details/911

Zernicke, Kate and Michael T. Kaufman. "The Most Wanted Face of Terrorism." *New York Times,* May 2, 2011, http://www.nytimes.com/2011/05/02/world/02osama-bin-laden-obituary.html

All Internet sites were accessed on December 13, 2017.

Index

About the Author

Emma Carlson Berne is the author of many biographies and books of history for young people. She lives in Cincinnati, Ohio, where she reads, rides horses, and runs after her three little boys.